All About Mummies

Dianne Irving

Contents

Mummies from Egypt

Maybe you have seen a picture of a mummy. Mummies have been made for thousands of years. In this book, we are looking at mummies from the country of Egypt.

an Egyptian mummy

Egypt is a hot, dry country in Africa. **Ancient** Egyptians made mummies thousands of years ago.

Some ancient Egyptian mummies were put inside the pyramids.

What Is a Mummy?

A mummy is a body that has been **preserved**. The ancient Egyptians wanted the bodies of people who had died to last forever. So, they preserved the bodies and made them into mummies.

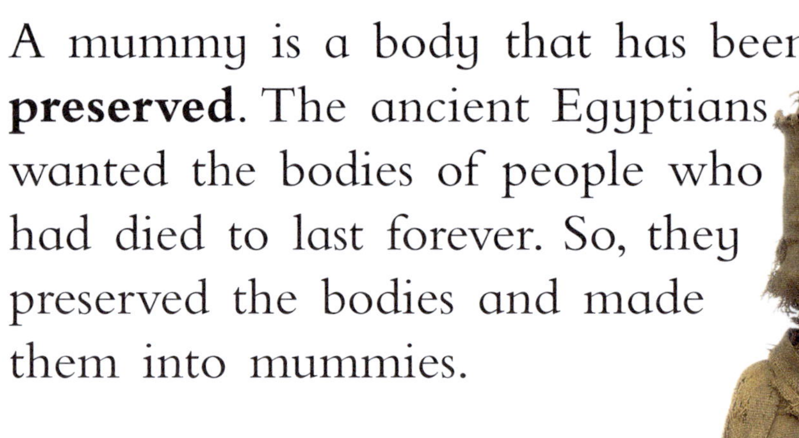

This is a mummy of a child.

This pot contains bandages. Bandages were used to wrap the body to help preserve it.

It took a long time and a lot of money to make a mummy. Not everyone was made into a mummy. People like kings or queens, or rich people, became mummies when they died.

a statue of an Egyptian queen

Why Make Mummies?

The Egyptians believed that there was another life after a person died. They called this the **afterlife**.

The bodies of people had to be preserved so they would be ready for the afterlife.

These Egyptians are giving a mummy gifts to take into the afterlife.

The Mummy-makers

Mummies were made by people who were mummy-makers. Their job was to turn a body into a mummy.

Making mummies was a very special job. The mummy-makers had to take care with all the parts of the body.

These men are wrapping a body in bandages to turn it into a mummy.

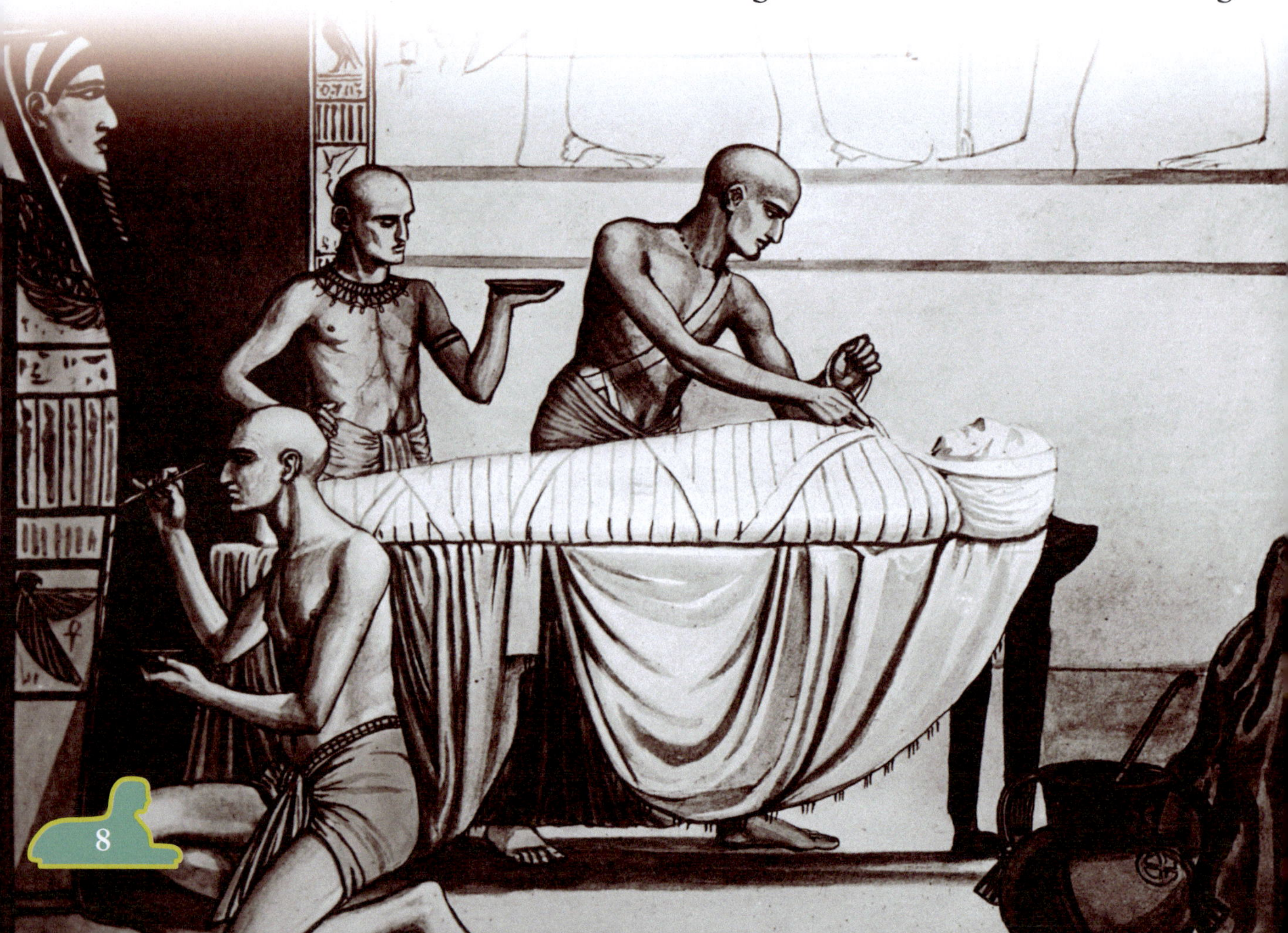

Turning a body into a mummy took a very long time.

Mummies were wrapped in bandages like these.

The mummy-makers took the bodies to a place called the Beautiful House.

a dead body at the Beautiful house

It took 70 days to make a mummy. First, the body was washed. Then, the inside parts of the body were taken out. Some parts were put into jars.

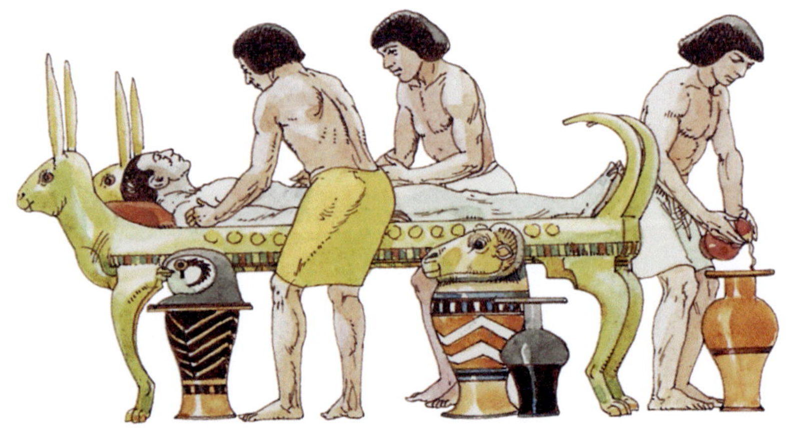

mummy-makers washing the body

Different body parts were put in these jars. The jars were then put with the coffins. The mummies were inside the coffins.

The mummy-makers put salt all over the body. This was to stop the body from rotting.

The body was left to dry for 40 days. Then, it was filled with **bandages**, salt and **spices**.

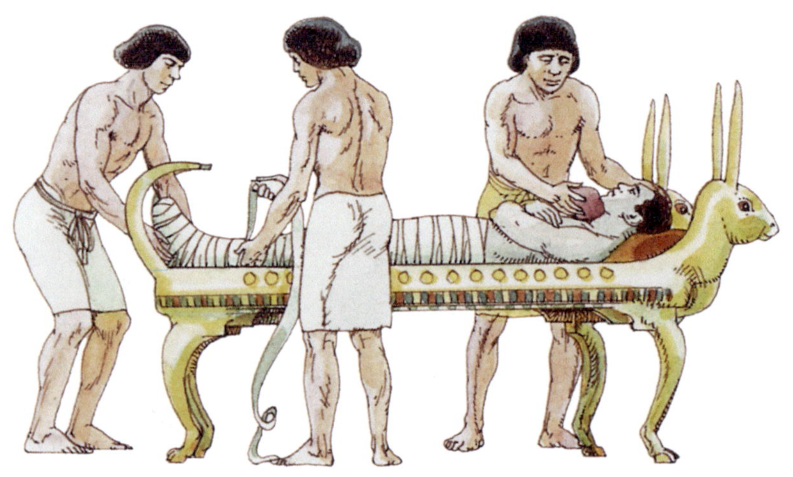

The last step was to wrap the body in bandages. Gold, jewels and wooden tags were placed in the bandages to **protect** the body.

a wooden tag

The mummy-makers did such a good job that many bodies are still preserved today!

The preserved mummy is inside this coffin.

The Egyptians believed that the body would see, hear, eat and drink in the afterlife. So food and drink was left with the mummy.

These men are leaving grapes, fish and other food with the mummy to take to the afterlife.

Sometimes, the mummy had a face mask.

A mask was put on the face of the mummy to protect the body's soul from evil spirits as it made its way to the afterlife.

Homes for the Mummies

When the mummy was ready, it was put into a **coffin**. The coffin was like a home for the body in the afterlife.

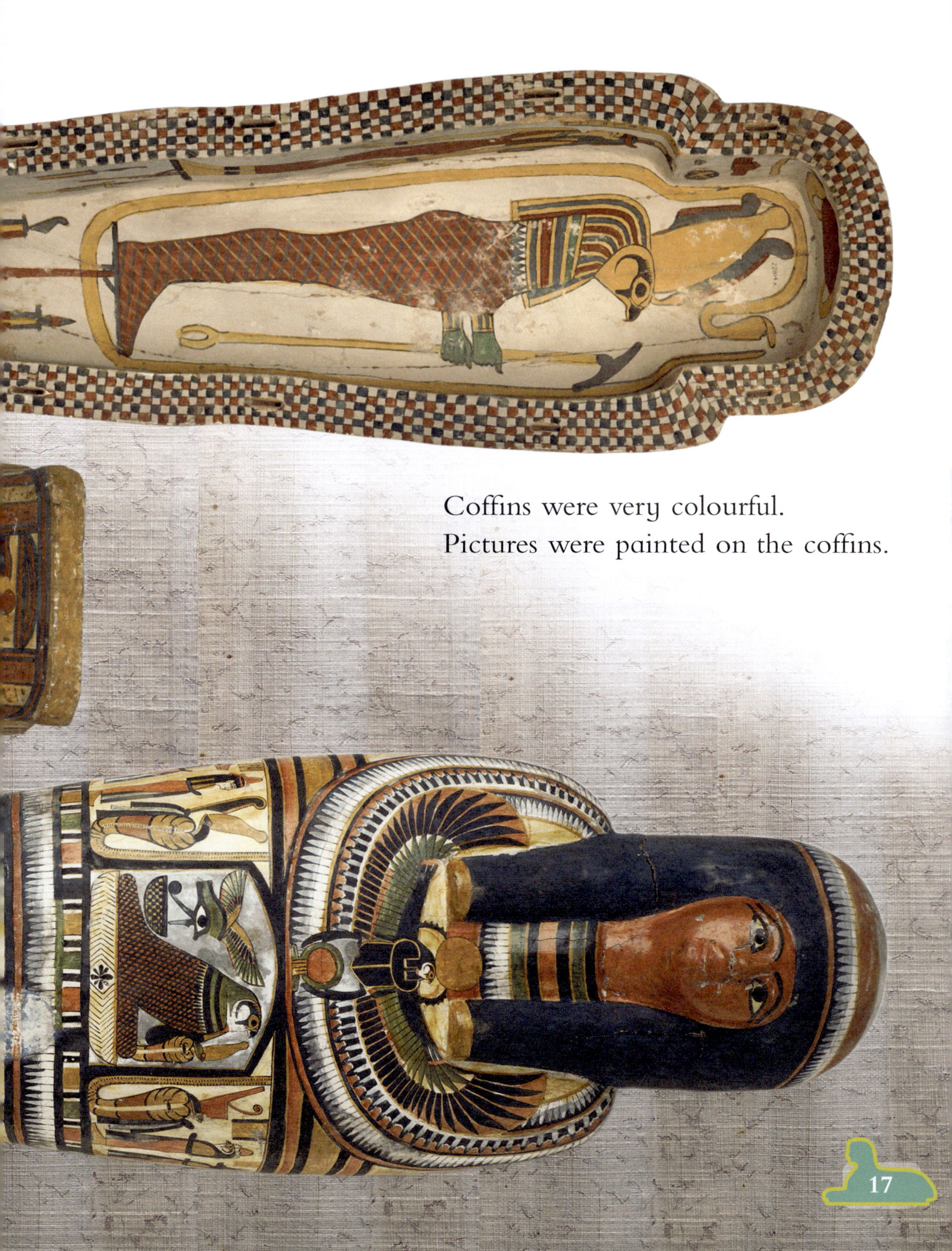

Coffins were very colourful.
Pictures were painted on the coffins.

Mummies of Kings and Queens

The kings and queens of Egypt were very important people. Some of the mummies of the kings and queens were put in gold coffins.

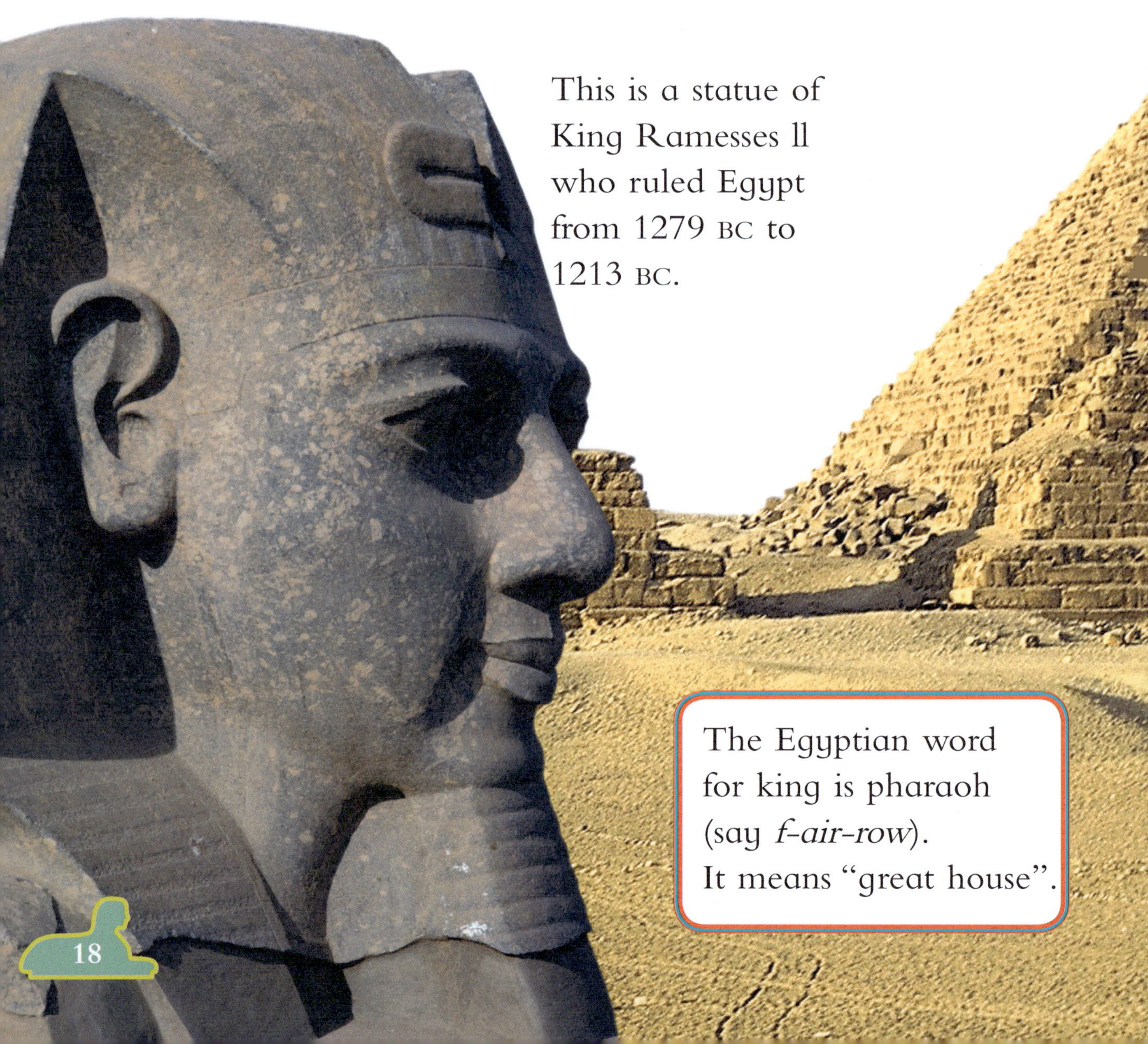

This is a statue of King Ramesses ll who ruled Egypt from 1279 BC to 1213 BC.

The Egyptian word for king is pharaoh (say *f-air-row*). It means "great house".

The gold coffins were put into the Great Pyramids.

King Tutankhamun

The most famous Egyptian mummy is Tutankhamun's (say *Toot-an-ka-moon*) mummy. This mummy was found in 1922. Tutankhamun was a young king. He became

the king when he was about 9 years old! He died when he was about 19 years old.

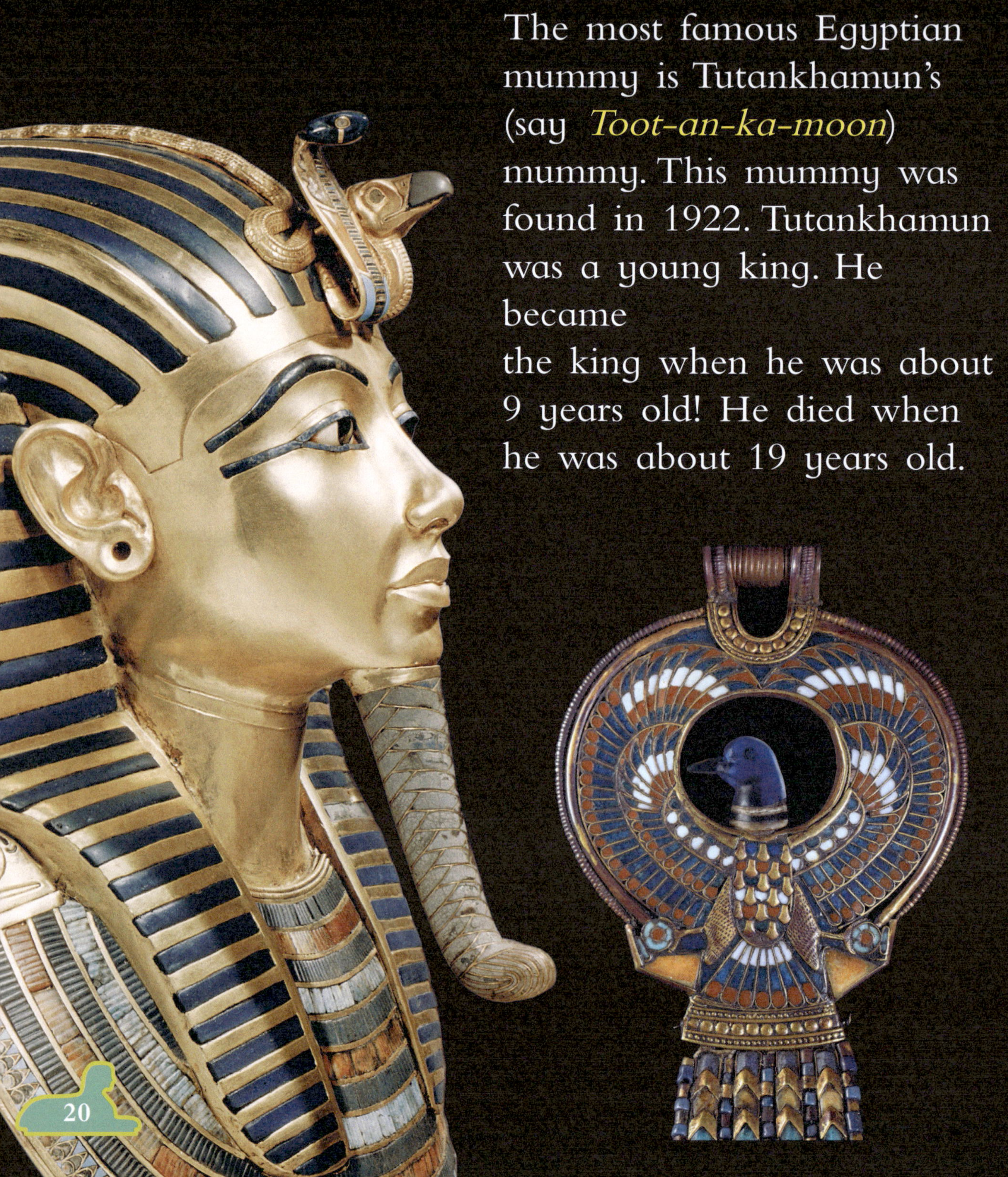

Tutankhamun's coffin was found in a room full of jewellery, gold chairs, musical instruments and other beautiful things.

King Tutankhamun's Mask

One of the most amazing finds was Tutankhamun's mummy mask. It was made from solid gold!

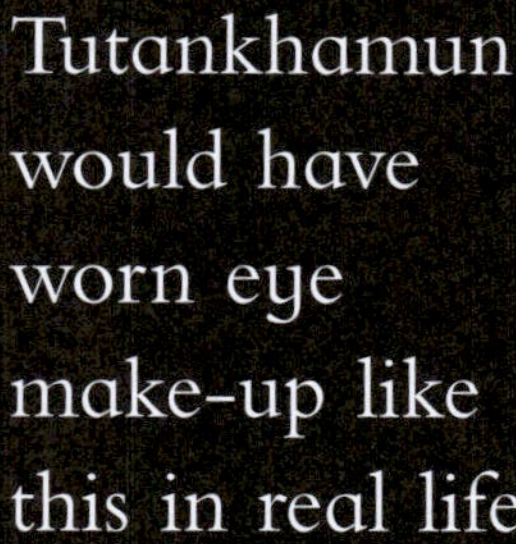

The vulture and the cobra stand for 'king' and 'protection'.

The mask weighs 11 kilograms.

The mask is 54 centimetres high.

Tutankhamun would have worn eye make-up like this in real life.

The beard is a symbol of a king or ruler of Egypt.

The face mask's collar is decorated with gold, coloured glass and semi-precious stones.

The mask's headdress is made from stripes of gold and glass that has been coloured dark blue.

Glossary

afterlife
another life after a person dies

ancient
from a time long ago, in the past

bandages
cloth wrappings

coffin
the box or case that a dead body is put in

preserved
stopped from rotting away

protect
to keep safe, look after

spices
food stuffs such as cinnamon